MW00415325

The Blind Broom Salesman

7 Life Principles for Abundance & Meaning

Barbara Atkins-Baldwin

The Blind Broom Salesman

Seven Life Principles for Abundance

Based on a True Story

Barbara Atkins-Baldwin

Copyright 2006

New Age, Creative Non-Fiction

4

Dedicated to my mother
"Your gentle spirit blows in the wind
And I hear your sweet voice
The touch of your hands are but a memory
A memory that will never be forgotten
Your beautiful face illuminated many hearts
Your accepting heart filled many souls
Judgment was never an option
Your life was scattered among a precious few
A precious few who will love you entirely
You have a heart of a child
Your innocence and trust your greatest virtue
I remember your laughter… it is part of me
I remember your fears… they are mine too
I remember your generous spirit... I am
grateful to give
I remember your independence… I am self-
sufficient
I remember the way you loved… I strive to
compare
Although you are gone now,
You are the source of my strength
You gave me compassion in your dying
You gave me understanding in your living

I look to the heavens and know you are there
I feel your love with me always… I know you
are near
Your gentle spirit blows in the wind and I hear
your sweet voice"

Table of Contents

Preface

Acknowledgements and Inspirations

For my inspiration:

Ernest Holmes, The Science of Mind

Deepak Chopra, The Seven Spiritual Laws of Success

Wayne Dyer, The Power of Intention

Catherine Ponder, Open Your Mind to Prosperity

Abraham-Hicks, Ask and It Is Given and the many messages of their workshops

For my teachers:

Micki Grimland, Life Coach and Therapist

Jesse Jennings, Teacher and Minister

For my support:

Chris Atkins-Barratt, for being the first to read this book, for being my home base and for sharing her family with me.

Preface

My background would be considered by most to be average. I cannot boast of high academic achievements. I don't carry a Ph.D. behind my name, nor am I famous. And yet, I feel called to tell this story.

There is a saying by Pierre Teilhard de Chardin (1881-1955), a visionary French philosopher. His quote transcends our understanding of our worldly journey: "We are not human beings having a spiritual experience; we are spiritual beings having a human experience."

It is with the heart of a child, the spirit of the wind, and the soul of a poet that I offer this book.

The story is based on a true story. The blind broom salesman is still selling brooms at the age of ninety as of the publishing date (2006).

The story is real; However, I have taken some liberty with aligning the story with the seven principles of prosperity by creating a few childhood encounters to illustrate these principles.

It is my strong belief that my mother crossed from the other side to co-author this book with me. It might sound far-reaching, but you see, my mother was an aspiring writer and although she was never published in her lifetime, her voice is finally heard in this story. She felt she had to have a Ph.D. before anyone would read what she had to say.

My mother went back to school after having her five girls, struggled to balance work and family, studied into the wee hours of many nights, dedicated herself to higher education, and after many years, completed her Ph.D. I remember being so proud of my "Dr. Mom."

I suppose she thought she would feel a sense of self-worth once she obtained high academic achievements, but she didn't feel worthy, and nothing coming from the outside can make one worthy,,, that's an inside job. She didn't realize that she was born worthy; it is just our thoughts that keep us from feeling it. Just a few short years after completing her Ph.D., her life ended. So the lesson for me is: don't wait to express the greatness that is in you.

Do not die with a song left unsung in your heart or a dance left in your steps. Live life fully, know you are worthy to take up space in this world, and step into that unique authenticity that is YOU. This book is not just my thoughts, but stories from a higher perspective, some call it the other side or Spirit.

As a sales person, the story of the blind broom salesman has inspired me to knock on more doors in a way that opens the doors to people's hearts.

The blind broom salesman reminds me to sell with integrity, honor, willingness, a sense of gratitude, and a feeling of being part of a whole. The Broom Man brings to mind recognition that there is something larger than myself working in the sales process.

I invite you to open your mind to the possibilities of greatness and to the realization that you have already achieved greatness. And as you read the sweet story of the blind broom salesman, know that everything you are or have ever needed is yours right now. You are capable of being your highest and best self at this moment. And in the blink of an eye, a life can change. I invite you to get to know The Broom Man and I hope he inspires you as he did for me so many years ago.

Chapter 1
The Story of the Blind Broom Salesman

Are you earnest? Then seize this very minute.
What you can do, or dream you can, begin it
with boldness and genius, power and magic in
it, only engage, then the mind grows heated.
Begin, and then the work will be completed.
-- Goethe

We always had several brooms in our house. Large ones, small ones, oversized ones, even little hand-sized brooms. All lined up, perfect straw bristles, bright red broom handles... a beautiful sight. Sweeping was never a chore with one of these brooms.

There was a sense that you were cleaning out your closets to make room for more good. There was a feeling you experienced every time you swept up the debris in your life with one of these brooms.

You may be wondering why I am telling you a story about brooms. Well, this is actually a story about a man who touched me – and touched many lives – and it is time his story was told.

When I was a small child there was a broom salesman that made house calls, door to door, and my mother was a repeat customer. What was unusual about this broom salesman was that he was blind. He was a graceful, soulful, elderly black man who went door-to-door selling brooms.

Six days a week he woke up at 6:30 and caught the bus one block from his home to take him to different parts of town.

The "broom man," as we called him, amazingly never got lost. He was quoted in an article once saying, "I don't want sympathy or to feel dependent, I want to be treated like everyone else." His ears, feet, sense of touch, sense of smell, and his cane were his eyes.

He walked around town, managing curbs and streetlights, and finding the front door to his loyal customers for more than forty years. In his mind he had no obstacles. In his mind there were no hurdles he had to overcome. There was no worry that someone might try to pay him with a ten-dollar bill and claim it was a twenty. He simply trusted the Universe and the people in it.

He knew that people, at their core, were decent loving people. That is not to say that he didn't get doors slammed in his face. Once a woman yelled at him and said, "Can't you read the sign? NO SOLICITING!" Then she proceeded to slam the door in his face. But this didn't intimidate the broom man. He knew a "no" was just one step closer to a "yes," and he moved on to the next opportunity.

Every day he visited a hundred homes and twenty-five to thirty businesses, covering eight to ten miles a day. You could even find him selling his brooms on cold winter days. The cold didn't seem to bother him; he was simply grateful to have good shoes and a warm coat on those days.

It is still a wonder to me that he could remember where all of his repeat customers lived, how many steps it was to the bus, the number of blocks to each customer, right turns, left turns. I suspect it was not just what we call memory; it was a deep knowing and a trust that he was held in the hands of God, and was absolutely and utterly safe – as we all are.

As a small child, I felt deep emotions when I saw him walking up our driveway. It was the strangest of feelings. It was a combination of gratitude, sweetness with a hint of sacredness. This felt very different than anything I had ever felt before, and so I watched his every move with heightened awareness.

When I would see the broom man coming up to our door, with eight to ten brooms thrown over his shoulder, confidently walking up our stairs with fresh expectancy, ringing the door bell, I knew this was more than a sales call. I somehow knew that this was a deep, soulful experience and an encounter that I would take with me the rest of my life.

I ran to the door when the doorbell rang, screaming "MOM! The broom man is here!" And my mother, my sisters, and I would listen to The Master Salesman effortlessly describe the quality of his brooms, always with a gentle smile and a self-assured belief. It was as if he could see them just as we saw them.

His fingers would glide across the top of the broom to show you how even the bristles were, his hands would wrap around the center of the broom bristles to show how tightly they were wound, and he would tell of the quality of the wooden handle as he turned it around and began to demonstrate by sweeping the ground.

He would talk of all the benefits his brooms brought to the buyer – like how they would get the job done quicker and cleaner with less physical effort. Oh he knew these brooms like one knows the back of our hand as he made them with his own hands. He was a salesman. Not a blind salesman. He was a Soulful Salesman.

The Broom Man brought with him a feeling, a higher intent beyond his product, and that is what we bought, the feeling -- the feeling that everything was right in the world. We bought the feeling that an encounter was more than a physical experience. An encounter with the Broom Man was a meaningful connection.

I watched my compassionate mother stop everything to listen intently to the broom man. I could sense that she felt a deep sense of peace as she listened to his "sales pitch." She was moved by his visits, beyond what she could explain. She didn't know why exactly her life was just a little sweeter after her encounter with him.

I'm not even sure if she was even conscious of what she felt while he was at our door, but I could sense it was a sort of relief, a small moment in time where the chores of the day were forgotten. It was a time to reflect on what was good in the world, and a time of gratitude.

My mother was an aspiring writer; I remember seeing her at her typewriter as she worked intently on a story about the broom man. One day, when the broom man appeared at our front door, she invited him into our home and had asked him if she could read him a story that she had written: "The Story of the Blind Broom Salesman."

We all sat around the dining room table as my mother began to read a poignant story about this "broom man" who touched her life in unexpected ways. It was an inspiring parable of will, determination, generosity, gratitude, compassion, willingness, cleaning out closets, intentions, spirituality, love, and acts of kindness.

As my mother read her story out loud to him in her soft gentle baritone voice, the blind broom salesman was visibly moved. Her five children witnessed an incredible expression of spiritual connection that day.

The broom man leaned forward in his chair, listening with the heart of a child to the story of his life and how his life made a difference. He listened to how maybe all these years he spent selling brooms was not wasted time. And maybe, just maybe, his life really did matter in a deep and soulful way.

He appeared to be so touched by this woman, my mother, and her kind-heartedness. And as I watched, a single tear rolled down his weathered cheek. Moved beyond words, he listened to the spoken words as if time stood still. As my mother read the last words, "And so, this man's life will live in my heart forever..." I looked at the blind broom salesman and saw a kind of softness in his face, a sort of release come over him.

I couldn't take my eyes off of his face. I kept staring at his eyes. People often say the eyes are the windows into your soul. I could not see into the broom man's eyes that day, and yet, all I could see was soul, a higher spirit, a divine being.

I witnessed the most beautiful moment in my life at that dining room table so many years ago and will carry that memory with me forever.

***

To this day, I carry that memory into my daily life. I am still touched by the life of the blind man. As a salesperson, a spiritual practitioner and a Corporate Business Sales Leader, I call on the memory of the blind broom salesman when I don't want to wake up at 4:30 in the morning to catch a plane to go on a sales call, or when I have any thoughts of lack. I think about this man when I am encountering so-called "hardships" or "obstacles" in my life. He is a source of my inspiration. For his life, I am deeply grateful.

The lessons I learned from the blind broom salesman are revealed in this book. You will see how the broom salesman's story is a metaphor for what I call the seven principles of prosperity. For the business person in each of you, or the part of you that seeks more meaningful connections, it is my hope that you might find how you can engage your spirit in your work in the pages that follow.

As you read through this book, you will find the following principles outlined and related to the story of the blind broom salesman:

1. We live in a Reciprocal Universe.

There is a power in living generously. It creates the consciousness that there is enough. When we understand the natural cycle of life that says, *what is planted, will grow, what is nurtured, will sprout, what dies will be reborn*, only then do we discover the secret of the universe. . There is a saying "In order to get, we must give". There is absolute truth to this. Acts of giving and a spirit of generosity shout to the universe that we are ready to receive. For every action there is an equal and opposite reaction and we can trust that the universe is mirroring our efforts in kind. Simply recognizing this principle and understanding that we live in an abundant universe prepares us to work from a space of generosity and trust.

2. Gratitude – What we are grateful for, expands.

What we are grateful for expands. If you want more love, be grateful for the love you already have in your life. If you want more money, be grateful for the money you do have. If you want a new car, be grateful for the one that gets you around today. If you want more sales, be grateful for the customer sitting in front of you. Gratitude creates a positive-flow consciousness, allowing our good to flow to us. Appreciating what you already have and feeling grateful right now activates the Universal Law of Attraction.

3. Cleaning out your closets and de-cluttering your life.

Using the metaphor of the mystical broom, we begin to clear out the clutter in our homes, garages, cars, and even the clutter in our minds and hearts. A space that is cluttered and filled with unused items literally carries "baggage" and negative energy. The process of releasing articles of clothing or items that have no meaning prepares the space for something new, physically and emotionally. The process of releasing others through forgiveness opens our hearts and minds to our greater good and the greater good of the world around us. Mental clutter of worry, false beliefs and negative emotions block any perception of abundance and in that way, literally prevent us from experiencing its reality. Sweeping out the clutter in our minds and lives will create a clean space to begin fresh. In this new uncluttered space, we find an energy and vitality we never knew existed.

4. Thoughts are things!

It is said our thoughts are like magnets. What you think about and the thoughts you focus on, is what you attract. Paying attention to your thoughts is the most powerful way to change your life. Everything that has manifested in your life or in the world began with a single thought. So we will look at how thoughts literally manifest what is in our lives. Thoughts of lack will create more lack. Thoughts of abundance will create more abundance. Thoughts of love create more love. It is truly that simple.

5. Look for the better feeling thought

Prosperity is a feeling. It may be a feeling of freedom, ease, joy, or abundance. Ask yourself how you would feel if you had the perfect job, the perfect spouse, the big sale, or the money to live financially free. Really feel the feelings of being totally embraced in this picture. If you can feel the feeling now, why not choose to feel this way until your picture is your reality. So if we change how we feel about something, we can change our belief

about it which will change our experience of
it.

6. *Live our dreams with intention*

To dream is to float on a river in the Mind of
God. Allowing yourself to dream creates the
desires of your heart. What if you dreamed
that you were walking on the beach, and when
you awoke, you had sand in between your
toes! A focused intent on the desired outcome
produces results and intention transforms your
ideas into reality. In all things set your
intention for the highest good of everyone
involved. Let go of *how* things get done and
trust that a dream only needs a dreamer.

7. *Love.*

Love is the opposite of fear, it is truly the only
thing that is real in this thing we call life.
Love transcends the physical life and elevates
our thoughts to create an abundant flow. Love
is a choice and not a feeling outside us. So
what if you said in the midst of heartbreak, "I

choose love;" what would happen to your experience?

Let's explore these principles more completely. I invite you into the life of the blind broom salesman from a child's perspective. And as like the mind of the child, there is creative liberty taken. As you journey through the principles of prosperity, my wish is it will send you on the road to a richer, more satisfying life.

Chapter 2
Prosperity Principle #1
We live in a Reciprocal Universe

While you have a thing it can be taken from you… but when you give it, no robber can take it from you. It will be yours always.
– James Joyce

"Money is like blood. It must flow. Hoarding and holding onto it causes sludging. In order to grow, it must flow. Otherwise it gets blocked and, like clotted blood, it can only cause damage."
– Deepak Chopra

About every six months the blind broom salesman visited our house, not surprisingly, just about the time our brooms needed replacing. The next visit after my mom had read the story to the blind broom salesman, I was eight years old and my grandfather had just died. I was sitting on the radiator next to the big picture window that looked out over our driveway. I was feeling melancholy about my grandfather's passing. I was day-dreaming as I often did, remembering going to our cabin with my grandfather and the many outings we'd had. I was remembering the time when I walked into a bait and tackle store with him.

I held onto his hand as we walked into the store, which always gave me a sense of belonging. As we walked into the old store we saw these kids who hung around the shop to get odd jobs. I remember I was feeling sad for these kids because they did not appear to have any money or much of any material things. So, just as I was going to give my bait to a boy who had a long look on his face, my grandfather pretended to be annoyed with all this "change in his pockets," and threw his change on the counter where several coins fell on the floor. I knew what he was doing.

It was his way of giving to these small boys without hurting their pride. He just had this way of giving at the right time, to the right person and for the right reasons. I looked up at my grandfather as I grabbed his hand and connected with his penetrating eyes, and without saying a word, we left the shop. Nothing needed to be said. I knew the boy with the longing eyes was able to buy bait and a coke that day, and was able to enjoy the entire day fishing at the local pond, a memory that I will cherish always.

And slowly as if waking up from a dream, I found myself back at my picture window. As I looked out the window, I saw the blind broom salesman walking up the driveway in his soulful way that always brightened my day. Although today, I didn't think the blind broom salesman could change my disposition. I got up from the window seat and walked to the side door to greet him.

There he stood at the door with a kind and gracious smile. I opened the door and said hello, my mother is not home today, and expected him to say he would come back when she is home.

Instead, he said, "Oh well, that's okay, do you know if she needs any brooms?" "I'm sure she does, but she didn't leave any money."

"Oh, that's not a problem; she's always good for it. She can pay me later.

You don't seem yourself today, are you okay?"

Caught off guard, I said, "Oh nothing, I'm fine."

The broom man gently spoke, "I heard that you lost your grandfather this week; could that be why you are feeling sad?" Tears filled my eyes and I acknowledged that indeed I had a terrible loss. "Your grandfather was a customer of mine. He was a good and generous man. He used to buy many brooms from me and we had such wonderful talks. He was a good and honest businessman.

It reminded me of a day I spent with him many years earlier when I visited him and he was making a big pot of stew and invited me in for a bowl. It was the lunch hour, and I was just about ready to break for lunch. I was so touched by his generosity. Your grandfather was known for that you know."

"Yes, I said, I know." And then the broom man said something that stayed with me for years to come. "Generosity is a state of mind you know, many people miss this. Generosity is equally about the gift of giving as it is about the gift of receiving gracefully.

Whenever you give your time, energy, spirit, and love to anything, you gift the world. Whether you are working for someone else or for yourself – like your grandfather did – you are giving. It is what I call the circular exchange of giving and receiving." He smiled wide. "What do you mean?" I asked. He said, much like when your mother buys a broom from me, not only am I getting paid for making brooms, but your mother is receiving a quality broom to do her cleaning. It is an even exchange of good. And your grandfather knew this secret." "It's a secret?" I asked.

"Well he paused, anyone can know the secret if they look deep inside their own heart. It is really about doing something you love, with love, from that place deep inside you. If you work and play from that happy place deep inside, you will live a prosperous and rewarding life. Consider your grandfather; he was rewarded a hundred fold with an abundance of friends, family and wealth."

"Yes," I said. "You should have seen how many people came to his funeral. The line of cars went on for miles and miles."

"Oh my, I bet that was a sight to see," he said. "That sure is a testament to the life he lived. Your grandfather never met a stranger, you know. He found ways to help everyone he met, even if it was just a moment of laughter. He embraced life and I know he benefited from the love he received in return. I know he loved you girls so much. I remember how his voice would soften when he spoke of you."

Somehow, the broom man got me to smile. It felt good talking to someone who knew my grandfather in this way. I asked him if he wanted to wait until my mother came home, or come back later. And he handed me a beautiful broom with a bright red handle and said, "tell your mother, I said hello, and that I was sorry to miss her this time around."
"But I don't have any money to pay you," I said.
"Oh that's all right; you have paid me by your company, your kindness and the memory of your grandfather."

"But, but... I ... I can't accept this broom without paying you!"

"The broom man said, "Remember what I told you about giving and receiving?"

" Yes, I remember, "I said.

"By giving you this broom today, it will make selling the rest of my brooms much easier. It will simply take less effort before my pockets are overflowing and all of my brooms are sold today; I guarantee you that. I like to think of it as there being only One bucket, One Giver and One Receiver. Giving, it seems somehow fills up my own bucket quicker. Some think that when you give, it is gone. Quite the contrary, it is a universal law that what goes up, must come down. What goes out must come back. What is given must be received. So tell your mother hello from me, and tell her I will see her next time.

"I will tell her," I said. "I know she will be sorry that she missed you; she enjoys your visits so much."

"Well," the broom man said, "I enjoyed our visit very much today and I hope you enjoy the rest of your day." And with that, he smiled kindly and walked down the stairs, across the driveway and disappeared down the street.

I watched as he carefully walked down the street, his cane as his eyes, until he disappeared into the distance. I was left standing there holding this beautiful red broom. And so, I began to sweep off the porch steps. There was this feeling that built up inside me as I thought of the words he'd said about giving, and like nothing I'd felt before, I felt I had a huge reservoir of energy inside me. I felt compelled to think of ways in which I could give back and pass along this message of giving.

After sweeping off the steps, I went inside to see what I could give. And I suddenly remembered mom had bought my favorite ice-cream bars, and they were in the freezer! I'm not talking about any ice-cream bar, they were the creamy vanilla ice-cream covered in rich milk chocolate bars. They were my all-time favorite. If I gave these away that would surely be a sacrifice for me I thought. So I set out on my journey. I got my little red wagon, filled it with sand from my sandbox (my other favorite thing), and put the box of ice-cream bars in my wagon.

I felt so inspired as I walked around the block and went up to each door. I tried to close my eyes to feel what it might feel like if I were blind. It was very difficult, and I had to often peek to see where I was going. After tripping a few times and walking off the side walk, I decided it might be best if I went about this journey with my eyes wide open. And so, I walked up the stairs to each house and I put a pile of sand at the front door, for in my mind, sand was the perfect platform on which to place an ice-cream bar. I carefully placed the ice-cream bar on top of the sand, and then proceeded to the next house on our block.

In my pure innocence and wonder, I was certain that each family would be elated as they opened the door to see this unexpected treasure!

***

Chapter 3

Second Principle of Prosperity
Being Grateful Expands Your Good

When you realize there is nothing lacking, the whole world belongs to you.   ---   Lao Tzu

It was the spring of my ninth year and it was a bright beautiful day in Nebraska. The cold winter had come and gone and the trees were in bloom again. The air was fragrant and the grass was turning greener with every breath I took. I loved this time of year and spent every moment I could outside just exploring, looking at a leaf, and digging in the damp soil. I thought about how distant the cold winter days seemed to me. I almost couldn't remember all the shoveling of snow, the winter boots, heavy coats, scarves and mittens that was needed to keep me warm. Winter was a distant memory now. .

As I lie in the grass out under a large oak tree, I looked up at the tree branches and the contrast of the green leaves against the deep blue spring sky. The new budding leaves seemed to grow before my eyes. The trees seemed to whisper to me something magical. I felt strangely connected to nature and the sweet fairies of spring. I couldn't see them, but I somehow felt they were watching over me. In a deep sense, I felt that this tree was my friend, a wise teacher. As I lie on the ground, and felt the cool grass beneath me, I imagined the roots of my tree growing very deep into the soil. I felt safe and comfortable and calm and very connected with the earth. There was no place I would rather have been in that moment. I closed my eyes for a few breaths and took it all in. As a smile appeared on my face, I heard a voice that said, "Now this is the way to spend a spring day."

I opened my eyes, and to my surprise, there was the broom man standing there with his brooms. He looked like a shadow from my position, almost like something larger was casting off the image of him. I sat up and said, "Hello! How did you know I was over here?"
"Oh, I felt the gratitude you were feeling and it drew me over here."

"How could you feel my gratitude?!" I exclaimed

"Well it is much like when you throw a pebble into a pond and the ripples in the water go out further and further until they reach the shore line. In the same way, feelings of gratitude ripple out until they are felt by another person. I simply felt the ripple of your gratitude. A life lived in gratitude is a life well lived," he said.

I was so happy to see him. I knew something magical was in store each time he visited. It was like time stood still during his visits.

"Well, I guess I was feeling grateful for the weather and stuff," I said.

"A funny thing happens in that place of gratitude. It reaches beyond things and stuff, and breaks into the space of pure possibilities. If you want more of anything in your life, start with being grateful for what you have. Be still, just like you are right now, and feel it in your heart, breathe in your good, know it is there and feel the gratitude in your heart. That is why it was so easy to spot you over here.

You must have been feeling grateful right down to your painted pink toenails!

Did you notice that when you feel grateful, it feels like there is nothing you need or want in that moment?"

" Well yes, I guess you could say I feel that way," I said.

"How can you feel that anything is lacking when you are feeling grateful for the abundance that nature has given us? Gratitude fills your entire self up. It just makes you feel *full*. I always say that prosperity and happiness are feelings, and the feeling of gratitude is the closest thing to a wealthy person."

" I see what you mean. I never really thought of it that way. That's a good way to look at it. Speaking of being grateful, my mother is home today, do you want me to go get her?"

"Oh, that would be very nice of you."

I took his hand and we walked to the front door. My mother was in the kitchen preparing lunch. And when she saw the broom man she turned and smiled and said, "Oh it is so good to see you today, how are you?" The broom man said, "Just fine, thank you. Will you be needing any brooms today?" "I certainly do, I have spring cleaning to do and the girls are going to help me, so I will need a few from you today."

I watched as my mother and the broom man made their exchange. I watched how he talked about which brooms would be best for each cleaning job. I watched the effortless exchange of words, gestures and money. I noticed how grateful both my mother and the blind broom salesman seemed in this moment. He was right about being grateful I thought, *being grateful makes you feel full.* I felt hungry for nothing in that moment.

After the exchange, the broom man said he must be on his way and thanked my mother for her purchase. He gestured with a tip of his hat and a smile and said to me, "Keep sitting under your tree. Be still and know that you have plenty. Be thankful for each breath, for each blessing, for nature, for your mom and each person in your life right now. Feel deep inside, a respect for nature and a sense of completeness. You are a child of the Universe, and have been given much. Your gratitude will expand the good in your life." And with that, he was out the door and onto the next encounter.

***

Chapter 4

The Third Prosperity Principle
Clean Out Your Clutter

Right thought, constantly poured into consciousness, will eventually purify it. Creation is the meditation of God.
-- Ernest Holmes

You all have a capacity for attraction, and when your process is clogged with stuff that you no longer want, the new attraction is slower.
-- Abraham/Ester & Jerry Hicks

I woke up ready for our annual spring cleaning day. The sun was shining, and it was a picture perfect day to open the windows and let the fragrant air of spring run through the house. The day was inviting me into its mystery. This was going to be the best day ever!

The air was fresh and had just a slight chill. The breeze was gentle and carried with it a feeling of new beginnings. The sun shone brightly into the windows and warmed all the empty spaces.

I ran downstairs to the broom closet, and saw the brooms neatly lined up in a row. There was a broom for each one of me and my sisters. The brooms were ready to be used, ready to take on the day. It was as if these brooms had personalities, stories to tell, wishes to grant, things to do and a purpose to express.

I don't know if it was that the brooms reminded me of the broom man, and his words of wisdom, or if they truly were touched with a bit of his magic. I thought about him and how he somehow made me feel better each time he visited, and I wondered if he'd left some of his special magic in his brooms. It didn't matter what was the literal truth, I knew in my heart, that these brooms held a certain mystical energy in them. I felt grateful.

As I looked at the brooms all lined up, I recalled true words of wisdom the broom man once told me, He said, "I like to think of these brooms as a symbol. The broom is a symbol for not only cleaning out the clutter in your house, but for cleaning out the clutter in your hearts and minds." He said, "Sometimes people have things that clutter their lives, like ancient hurts, long-held resentments and deep regrets." He said softly in almost a whisper, "Let the broom remind you to forgive.

As you sweep out and clean your house, take a moment to sweep out and clean your heart and mind of any clutter that keeps you from living life fully. You will find that there is magic in forgiveness and grace in choosing love over all else."

I thought as I was cleaning out my closets – if I did it with love, I could create a feeling, a sort of energy that welcomes our guests and nurtures their spirits. Our guests will not know exactly why they feel better; they will just know that paying us a visit is somehow good for their soul.

I heard again the words of the broom man, "Cleaning out clutter and making open, clean spaces creates a flow, an integration and harmony of many things coming together for your good. That is the balance of being in the flow of life and the pursuit of your soul's expression."

As I stood there staring at the brooms, and remembering the words of the broom man, there was one broom that seemed to draw me to it. It was a little smaller than the rest, the perfect size for me. It seemed to fit perfectly in my small hands and I felt energized by the bright red handle.

I set out to sweep the front porch and began sweeping. I swept out every corner and crevice, all the while thinking happy thoughts. I thought about who might have built this porch back in 1910, and suddenly felt their presence around me.

It was as if these long passed spirits were smiling down on me, happy that their craftsmanship was being cared for. I felt connected to the families that shared loving moments in the past on this porch, I felt every happy moment that was ever felt by anyone in this one single moment in time. I could see grandparents rocking in their rocking chairs and parents reading to their children. I could hear the whispers of the past and children's laughter. I could see and feel a sense of family, gathering. I could smell the flowers long since bloomed and faded away.

Was this my imagination? Could this possibly be? How could I feel something or someone that was no longer living? I certainly didn't have all the answers, but I learned to trust my feelings. My mother once said that my intuition was always right. And somehow, this little red broom taught me about trusting these feelings. The broom man was right - these brooms did serve a higher purpose than simply cleaning out closets – if you allowed them to.

I felt a sense of belonging in this moment. I could see and hear families from long ago who'd lived before us in this home. I could feel the pain and sorrow of loss and disappointment and the bond of family that lifted the veil of long held hurts.

I could hear the laughter of my own sisters as we roller-skated across the tiled porch and our proud parents watching in awe as we mastered the art.

Yes, this was a magical broom! I will never know if it was the broom that surfaced all these visions and feelings or if it was the process of cleaning out the clutter. It doesn't really matter, all I know is that I felt the magic in this moment, and trusted it.

* * *

Chapter 5

Fourth Principle of Prosperity
Thoughts are Things
The Law of Attraction

There is nothing either good or bad, but thinking makes it so. -- Shakespeare

It is done unto you as you believe. – Jesus

Thoughts are things. – Ernest Holmes

Spring had long passed. The summer winds came and went. The red and orange leaves had fallen from the trees and had made a blanket of beautiful rich colors on the ground. And it came time once again where a winter chill filled the air. The trees are barren and yet you know that this is the time when the roots are growing deeper and the tree is becoming stronger. It is a time of year to go within-- within your homes to stay warm, and within your heart to reflect on life and love.

I'd had another birthday and was ten years old now. It was holiday break from school and I was thinking about what the day had in store for me. There was a fresh blanket of snow on the ground, and this brought many opportunities for the day. I could of course, shovel the sidewalk and driveway, I could get the new sled and go sledding, or I could make a snowman that looked so real, that it would stop people in their tracks. Oh, this was a good day! Since my father was already outside with the snow-blower, I had decided that making a snowman was my first priority. I ran downstairs and put my new snow space boots on. You know the kind – with the bubble-looking Michelin tire man look. I wrapped my face and neck with a warm scarf that my grandmother had made, and reached for my stylish hat that had a long tail with a big red ball at the end of it. I retrieved my mittens from the radiator and felt their warmth as I slid them over my cold hands. I waved to Dad, gave him a big smile and ran to the front yard to build my masterpiece.

Where should I begin? I started with just a little snow ball and carefully placed in on the ground and began to roll it over the newly fallen snow. It was perfect, the sticky kind of snow, just right for making snowballs, and as I rolled my little baseball-sized snowball into a massive boulder that I could barely roll with my entire body, I had noticed that I had made a grass trail where my snowball had rolled. Almost like the snowman had walked up to this spot.

Oh, this was perfect ! I had a large round base that would hold my middle section just perfectly. And so I began again, making a snowball with my hands and rolling and rolling until it was just slightly smaller than the one before. It took all the strength I had to pick it up and put it on top of the base. Ah, yes - perfect! My snowman was coming together just as I had imagined.

I was in the snowman zone, that frosty the snowman Zen state as I was making my little creation. My father had finished snow blowing and there was a silence in the air, almost a sacred feeling, like when you walk into the woods, the kind of silence that comes right after a snow fall. The kind of silence where you could almost hear a snowflake hit the ground. The air was so still and it felt like time was standing still.

Nothing else seemed to matter - it was just my thoughts and me now. I began to make the final snowball for the head and face. I rolled it just right and patted it and rubbed my hands around the snow, making it into a perfect round ball, just the right shape and size.

It was now time to accessorize – I was like an artist with a blank canvas. I envisioned exactly the way he would look when I was done, and could feel the energy of the Spirit of all snowmen that went before. I had begun to feel quite warm, so the first thing I did was to remove my scarf and put it around the snowman's neck.

Something stirred in me as I did this, the beginning of life, I thought. I ran over to the bushes and dug around for some broken branches to use as arms. I found two perfect branches that were like arms you would see in a Christmas card picture. Yes! Just as I had imagined they would be. I ran inside to get a carrot for his nose and charcoal for his eyes and mouth, I even found one of my grandfather's old pipes and a top hat of his. I grabbed an old pair of mittens from the utility room and rushed back outside to dress my new friend.

I carefully placed the charcoal eyes and made a big smile with the rest of the charcoal. The carrot was the biggest I could find and I placed it right in the center of his face. I put the mittens on the end of the sticks I had found and topped it off with a beautiful blackish-grey top hat. I thought for a moment that the snowman might come alive as I put that "old top hat" on his head, and thought he might begin to dance around as the song says.

Just as I put the top hat on his head, I heard a crunching in the snow; it was the sound of foot-steps. It startled me for a moment as I thought the sound was actually my snowman coming alive, then I looked over my shoulder, and there was the broom man walking up the sidewalk carrying his brooms with a smile.

"Looks like that snowman might need a broom!"

I thought, *How in the world did he know I had built a snowman?* I was convinced that he had eyes somewhere. My mom used to talk about a "mind's eye." *Maybe his mind had an eye,* I thought.

He walked up to the snowman, felt the snowman with his hands and said "Boy oh boy, that is a fine snowman you have built, right down to his nose. That is exactly how I would build a snowman if I were making one." And then he took one of his brooms and placed it near the snowman's right hand, just as if he were holding it. It was just right. I stood there and laughed with joy.

"Thank you! It's the perfect touch. How did you know I was building a snowman and where exactly to put that broom?"

"I knew this snowman would be here before I even got here. He said, in that wise tone, somewhere between a hush and a deep whisper, there is a power that creative thoughts carry; thoughts are like magnets, thoughts attract whatever you are thinking, thoughts create things. Literally, *thoughts are things.* Some people call it the Law of Attraction. Thoughts carry an energy that can be felt and seen by others. You must have been very focused about making this snowman, and my mind just got on the same ride as your creative thought wave."

"What do you mean you caught my thoughts?" " It is kind of like when I think about my day. I imagine all the people I will meet that day. I see each encounter, the route I will take, and I feel the joy of a perfect selling day. I don't think about even the possibility of not selling my brooms. I don't worry if people are going to pay me the right amount. I just know they will sell before I set one foot outside my front door. I don't let *what if* questions creep into my thoughts. Like what if I don't have enough money to pay my bills or, what if no one buys my brooms today, what if I miss my bus, what if, what if, what if. It happens to all of us. Our thoughts never stop.

Our thoughts are continually creating our life experiences. You see, we are the co-creators in our lives. We have this incredible opportunity to meet grace everyday. We can welcome the kindness of strangers, welcome the gratitude in their voice and that brings meaning to life."

"When you set out to build your snowman today, you must have had a vision of your snowman already completed. Did you notice how effortless it was to make the snowman?"
" Well, now that I think about it, the snow was sticky and just right for making snowmen. I found the sticks for his arms almost too easily. It was the easiest snowman I had ever made!" I exclaimed.

"That is because you already saw it done before you began."

So that was the secret! I didn't realize I had actually thought about the snowman and even imagined what it would look like once it was done." *Hmm, that was funny,* I thought.

I always wondered how he sold his brooms everyday. I suspect he knew that his sales would come effortlessly, that his customers would be there to greet him, that he would sell all of his brooms and that he would be touched in some way each day. And he was. Whether it was a heartfelt story a mother who had written about his life or simply a gesture of gratitude, he knew he would bump into his good each day and held that expectation, because he was in the Divine Flow of life.

Chapter 6

The Fifth Principle of Prosperity
Get the Feeling

"Let yourself be silently drawn by the stronger pull of what you really love." "Where-ever you are, be the soul of that place"
- Rumi

The rich soil that lay dormant during the winter and then bloomed the bright red and yellow spring tulips was now absorbing the summer sun. It was my summer break of my eleventh year and I found myself laying in my back yard, as I often did, feeling the cool earth beneath me. I had the whole summer ahead of me and a feeling of surrender and freedom had settled into my bones.

I lay there with my eyes closed, and noticed that when I closed my eyes, the sound of birds was so crisp and clear that it sounded as if they were inches from me. I took in a deep breath and noticed the rise and fall of my stomach with each breath, I could feel the clothing against my skin, and smiled knowing that I was wearing my favorite rainbow t-shirt.

I could smell the fragrant flowers and lush green grass that filled the air all around me. The colors were brighter in my mind than I remembered. I suddenly felt as if I was in a far away place, only my imagination could take me. It was a place where my soul came alive. Everything was brighter, more colorful. A sense of ease came over me. I could see, in my minds eye, my whole life in front of me, yet there was only this moment that mattered. If I could live in this moment, right now, that was all there was.

The sad feelings about my parents divorce did not exist in this moment. The ache I felt in my heart of my mothers absence could not be felt, only the feeling of the earth's cool embrace pounded in my heart. The uncertainty of a new step mom was replaced with the steady wave of the summer breeze. I felt I belonged here. I had a deep sense that I had been here before and that in a deep way, I was somehow of the earth and yet I was of something much larger too.

Everything and nothing was happening all at once. I felt the vibration of the earth in all that was and now is; feelings of love and hate, new beginnings and sad endings – all came together in this one place – it was all the same feeling. Neither good nor bad – just there, present in this moment of clarity and simplicity.

All my worries and cares seemed to just dissolve into the earth. It was as if my heartbeat was beating to earth's rhythm – it felt as if something larger than me was beating in my heart. It felt peaceful and easy.

As I lay there, my heart slowly beating, my eyes closed, and my mind's eye seeing beautiful rainbow colors and lush green fields, I heard a voice say out loud *"Summer dreaming"*. I thought it was my voice at first, and then recognized the familiar tone of that voice and knew the broom man was paying another visit.

I opened my eyes, smiled and said, hello – funny, I said- you always seem to find me out here daydreaming. *That is funny, I guess your joy just draws me to your house.* I asked how can you feel my joy? *Well, I feel it in my gut, it is hard to explain.* He didn't have to explain – when my eyes were closed earlier, I could feel the earth, the wind, my ancestors who lived and breathed before me, and every feeling that had ever been felt, so I kind of understood what he was saying. Do you think that because you are blind, you can sense these things more?

I think anyone can sense these things if they try. I think if more grown-ups would come lay down in the grass and feel the awe and wonder of Nature, and feel the Spirit of where they came from, we would all benefit from it. When we close our eyes we can remember times when we felt completely secure, cared for and content. We feel a sense of calming peacefulness that fills our heart. Did you notice how your body feels lighter when you daydream? In these moments, there is no need for a million dollars, a lavish vacation, or the latest new toy because what you seek is the feeling, and right now you have this feeling.

I've heard it said that form follows feeling. If we can begin to feel prosperous and free we open the floodgates and the flow of good into our lives. I sat there and soaked up his words of wisdom. He went on to say;

What would happen if we converted our thoughts and feelings of not enough, into feelings of abundance? Or what if we turned our feelings of unworthiness into feelings of belonging, or our feelings of envy into feelings of appreciation? No circumstance changes on the outside, the change simply happens in our own mind and imaginations, and suddenly, it changes our entire experience.

There are times in life when sadness feels like the only option. And I say do something physical that makes you happy. It might mean coming out and laying in the grass, or it might mean dancing in your living room. And I see that you know this secret already. I guess so. *You guess so?* I mean, I know so. *I thought so. I could feel that you knew.*

Did you ever notice when you close your eyes, there is something mysterious that takes place in the darkness. It is not really darkness is it? There is all forms of shapes and colors in that darkness, isn't there? The colors, smells and feelings of that place we call our imagination. We see this place inside us where creativity is born. We see a place where we feel the deepest feelings. We embrace this place, where deep inside our souls we come alive. That is exactly what I was experiencing earlier! *Ah, I said you already knew the secret. Just keep doing it; never grow out of it okay?*

Okay, I replied.

You probably want to see my mother. *You mean your step-mother?* I didn't know he knew my parents got a divorce and that I was now living with my Dad and Step-mom. *I talked to your mother. She said that it was the hardest thing she had ever done in her life, but she felt that having two parents and staying in this house would be better than moving into an apartment with her.*

I would have moved into an apartment if I knew that she wasn't going to be able to tuck me in each night. I miss her so much. *Yes, I know. Your mom loves you very much. You know that, right?* Yes I know that. *Your step-mom is a good person too. She only wants the best for you girls.* Yes, I know she does. I'm just sad that we can't be a family like we used to be. *Well you can still be a family. It will just look a little differently. Your mom is with you every time you close your eyes. You can feel her love surround you, just like I felt your feelings of joy earlier. She is only a thought away.* Somehow I knew this. I was pleased to hear the blind broom salesman confirm this for me.

Speaking of my step-mom, she is inside cleaning – I'm sure she could use one of your brooms today. *I'm sure she can too. You keep daydreaming and using your imagination the way you do, and you'll be alright.* And with that, the blind broom salesman was headed towards our front door.

Chapter 7

The Sixth Principle of Prosperity
Living Your Dreams

Inherent in every intention and desire is the mechanics for its fulfillment... And when we introduce an intention in the fertile ground of pure potentiality, we put this infinite organizing power to work for us. – Deepak Chopra

I was halfway into my summer break and it was a hot, hot summer day. You could have fried an egg on the sidewalk that day. The kids were playing outside in a flowing fire hydrant trying to cool off from the day. The neighborhood was buzzing with kids on their bicycles and just enjoying the summer fun.

I thought to myself, this was a perfect day to have a lemonade stand! Growing up in a family of entrepreneurs and business owners – running my own little enterprise was in my blood. I got so excited of the thought of building just the perfect lemonade stand, picking the perfect location and designing a powerful marketing campaign that I couldn't wait another minute. I ran downstairs and enlisted my little sister to join my team.

I was determined to have the worlds-best lemonade stand, I saw people standing in line around the block. I had always dreamed of owning my own business, and this was my opportunity to shine. I had already convinced my father to bring home a barrel of lemons from the market. This lemonade stand was going to be the real deal. No artificial flavors, nothing bought in a can - real lemons, real sugar, the good stuff.

I assigned my little sister to the creative marketing and product development division. She would make the poster-board signs for the stand, flyers and she was in charge of getting the product ready for sale. I was in charge of PR, marketing, and money. We had a solid plan, I was pumped. My sister had made creatively bright and colorful signs that said "Lemonade for Sale ... 25 cents". I had passed out flyers covering a 3-block radius.

We had done all the work to have a successful lemonade stand. And it was! A huge success! We couldn't keep up with all the demand, so I enlisted a few of the kids just hanging around watching our enterprise. They were happy to join such a successful endeavor. Everyone worked in harmony - we were laughing and having the time of our life.

We were so busy - I barely noticed the smiles on my customer's faces. My head was down, pouring the lemonade and making change, when I noticed a weathered black hand put a quarter into the palm of my hand and heard a that familiar voice say; *you sure picked a perfect day to sell lemonade!* I looked up and smiled at the broom man and said I was so glad to see him. I handed the change drawer to my sister and our selling team, and said I would be right back. I reached for the broom man's arm and said, come sit over here with me and drink your lemonade. *Ah yes, that sounds lovely he said.* We sat down under a shade tree and I watched as he slowly drank his glass of lemonade.

I heard the neighbors talking blocks away about this lemonade stand, you sure did a good job promoting. It was always a dream of mine to have a successful business, I said.

It's great to have a dream isn't it? When I think of people's dreams, I think about the oak tree that sleeps in the acorn, or the bird that waits in the egg, the gift that is yet to be given, and the child that is yet to be born. Dreams are the seedlings of life. So, dream big! A burning desire to be and to do something is the starting point from which the dreamer must take off. All great inventions, and accomplishments started out in the individual mind as a dream. So keep staring out that window and day-dreaming. A deep desire wrapped around a simple thought is what creates our world...

Pay attention to those little thoughts that won't leave you. It might be a desire to paint, sculpt, have a lemonade stand, or making a new friend... It is a yearning deep inside. It is your soul calling out to you. I say take action on those dreams – they are being given to you, and only you. Desire means "of the father". It is a Divine calling for your highest good. Life is meant to be lived. So pay attention to these inner-callings and take action however big or small.

He said something about sculpting, and that sounded like something I've always wanted to do – and I really wanted more friends too. I said to the blind broom salesman, sometimes it seems so hard to make new friends and do the things I dream about.

Simply just being willing to take a step towards your dream is the first step. What if I was neutral about selling my brooms. Do you think I would sell very many? Growth happens when you are willing. Willingness implies that you have overcome inner resistance to life and are committed to participating. When you are willing to do the work, people become genuinely friendly, and social and economic success seem to follow automatically. Willing people are builders of, and contributors to our lives.

I asked if I could get him another cup of lemonade, and he said he needed to be on his way but that he felt refreshed and ready to finish his day with a renewed vigor. He thanked me for the lemonade and handed me a broom to give to my mother. I paid him out of our lemonade money drawer and thanked him for his patronage. And with that, he was off.

Chapter 8

The Seventh Principle of Prosperity
In all things, Choose Love

I Am Life. I am not something apart from your being. I am your being. I Am the Truth, dispelling all error. I Am Power, neutralizing all weakness. I Am Abundance, swallowing up all lack. I Am your Real Self. So Recognize that your good is inside, you were born with it – it is only our thinking otherwise that keeps us from it.

-- Ernest Holmes, Living Science of Mind

And so, we visit for one last time the life of the broom man. Close your eyes once more, and imagine a light radiating from the center of your heart. It fills your entire body and begins to radiate outside your body. The light grows bigger and bigger, soon it fills up the room, your entire home. The light expands into the city and flows out into the world. This light is Pure Divine Love.

Unconditional Love welcoming all differences.

The Broom man radiated this light of love out into the world to greet him. Imagine for a moment, the broom man finding stillness every morning to feel the warmth in his heart and feeling his heart expand into his entire house, then beyond his walls and into the city. Before he arrived at any of his customers doors that day, he knew there would be a sense of heartfelt acceptance, warmth and love to greet him. He knew that his customers would feel this incredible sense of peace, calm and love. He knew this because there is a

Universal Law of attraction that says anything you focus on you attract. He sent out the light of love, and like a magnet, the light came back to him like a boomerang.

The unexplained feelings I had as a child when he would come to our door, were the feelings of love that he sent out before him. I felt that Universal Love that children can so easily sense. I would even anticipate his coming. Could I have felt the energy of love before he even got there? Yes!

Without question, I now know that love is a powerful energy and can be sent out to comfort with just a mere thought of it. There is innocence about it all. There is simplicity about sending out love to greet you in the world. The broom man had the market cornered when it came to selling love. He knew it was the magic in his brooms. If he would be completely upfront about his sales pitch, he would say, this broom was made with my own hands, and every bristle is infused with the love. But somehow he knew that he didn't need to put it into words, as this might create doubt. The individual experience of love was more powerful than his words, and he knew that.

Imagine a cold winter day in Nebraska, the driveway needs to be shoveled, the cars need a jump start, there is ice on the road and a chill in the air. And in a moment of grace, your doorbell rings, and there stands a man selling his brooms.

You're thinking possibly at first that this is the last thing you need, but something tells you to stop for a moment, listen to what he has to say. And suddenly your heart is filled with warmth that you can't explain. You feel a sense, well you don't want to call it "love", but it feels like a sweet embrace. It feels like you just sat down in front of a warm fire to drink a cup of hot chocolate, and so you are drawn to this feeling. You listen to this man and notice he is blind, but that is not what you really see. You realize this is a spiritual experience, it is bigger than you. And all this is felt because one man before he set out on his journey that day, set the intention to send out love for the souls he would encounter that day, and have love greet him at every door. One man decided to choose love. There were many choices available to him; racism, exhaustion, blindness, lack, poverty, hatred, and fear. But the only obvious choice to the broom man was love, kindness, respect, honor, compassion, empathy, freedom and joy. And that simple choice created his experience, and the experience of every one he encountered.

***

Chapter 9

Lessons Learned

What we expect, that we find – Aristotle

What we wish, that we believe. – Demosthenes

You were born with potential.
You were born with goodness and trust.
You were born with ideals and dreams
You were born with greatness
You were born with wings.
You are not meant for crawling, so don't.
You have wings.
Learn to use them and fly.
-- Rumi

I have often thought over the years of my sales career how effortless the blind broom salesman made selling his brooms seem. And having experienced many effortless transactions, I am convinced that when I am in deep gratitude for what I do have, I notice that selling becomes more about connections.

I am grateful for the customers I get to encounter, for the opportunities to connect with other spirit-beings and for knowing that there is meaning in every transaction. There are no coincidences when you think about all the potential customers you could meet.

It is not by chance you are sitting in front of a particular customer. If you are grateful for these seeming happenstances, you exchange an energy flow that vibrates at a higher level, and is it no longer about the sale – it is about being grateful for what you already have.

I often think about these times in my childhood when I allowed magical thoughts to enter my day. As a sales person today, I always pay attention to my sales flow, and recognize when sales are slow, it is usually because I have clutter somewhere in my life that needs attention. The clutter doesn't always mean a messy desk or an over-stocked bookshelf, it is often subtle clutter like a certain feeling. It might be feelings of worthlessness, resentment, pride or self-criticism that need some cleaning out. It might mean cleaning out the spaces in my heart that blocks my passion for what I am doing. It might mean organizing my thoughts and being willing to do the work that needs to be done in front of me.

Selling is a constant reminder to pay attention to what is going on in your mind and to do some spring-cleaning when things are slow.

When I think about specific times in my life that things have seemed to flow most easily, times when I have been gifted with success in love or in my career, I recognize that most often, these have been times when I set out with a clear picture in my mind of what I most wanted. I was feeling joyful, successful and at ease. All of my thoughts were about ease, success and peace.

Paying attention to my thoughts and the way I am feeling is the most important thing I can do and is the best training I could attend. When I find myself thinking that life is too difficult or that work is hard, or that there are more important things in life than the work in front of me, I stop and try to remember a time when I felt joy or a time when all things came easily.

I try to remember that everything in life has a purpose. My work flows to and from me in an effortless way like a boat floating downstream. I try to be aware that my thoughts are creating the world I live in. I choose to be in alignment with good thoughts and feelings. It is when I follow my bliss, that I am most happy. And in these times of thinking good thoughts, I witness success in my life.

These concepts are easier said than done! There are times in my sales career when I felt that I would never make another sale as long as I lived. Fortunately, I knew the secret. Granted, sometimes I would forget the secret for extended periods of time, but once I remembered it, magic would happen. If I find myself in a slump, I just close my eyes and remember the feelings of a time when all was well. I remember when sales were flowing in with ease. I remember the feelings of confidence that welled up inside me. The mind doesn't know the difference between reality and thoughts wrapped in feeling. I conjured up the feelings I once felt, and magically the energy would shift and I once again create a successful flow.

Staying in a state of bliss takes no less than practice. It starts by noticing how you are feeling. If you feel bad, you are not in alignment with your highest purpose. Remember the good feelings. Write them down if you have to. Make a vision board if that works. Keep a gratitude journal. Whatever it takes to access your good feelings, do it.

And so I find this new-found appreciation for the blind broom salesman. He walked through his life having a heightened sense of aliveness, connection to his feelings and senses. Feeling his way through his day, he walked his path with purpose, love, and deeply felt gratitude. Literally, feeling his surroundings gave him a sense of security. Figuratively, feeling a sense of confidence, connection and compassion with himself and the people in his life created a sense of awe and wonder that could be felt deeply by him and others.

Living a life full of wonder, full of deep felt connections was the motivation behind his actions, and this became my motivation too.

What is your soul's intention? What desires of the heart have been knocking at your door?

Ask yourself if you are willing to leave this planet with a song left unsung in your heart. Sing your song! No one else can sing it like you. It is meant to be sung.

I hope you live your song and dance your dance. And so dear reader, are you willing? Dreaming is energy in motion. What thoughts or activity can you engage in that will shift the energy that surrounds you into a positive flow of your good? Maybe you might make a list of actions and notice how you feel about them. Possibly paying attention to the feeling and what it is teaching you. Keep moving forward. Honor yourself by keeping your commitments. If you feel an urge to create, act on it. Be committed to your work. Find the joy, meaning and spiritual connection and get busy co-creating your life.

And for the sales person in each of you, I encourage one to tap into their authentic passion, the thing that lights up their life. Find out why you do what you do. Is it recognition for a job well done? Is it the money that brings a sense of freedom in your life? Is it the connection you feel with your co-workers or customers? Know deep down that you are co-creating and that when you follow your bliss, the rewards are great.

I grew up my entire life having the blind broom salesman sell my family brooms. Even now, in my forties, he is still alive and sweeping up souls. The blind broom salesman taught me about so many things, but mostly about being willing to do my work with integrity and love. I carry that spirit with me into my work and my life today.

Harvard University conducted experiments on the power of love, and how if applied, could cure most of the world's ills. The reason it works is because the love concept is so powerful that when it precedes your interactions, all disharmony falls away.

I am always in awe of this universal law. I attempt to practice the art of sending out this energy before any of my business meetings or causal interactions of the day.

Just like the butterfly effect of a butterfly's flapping its wings can be felt across the oceans, thought energy can have the same effect. The thoughts one sends out on the miraculous thought energy highway of the universe. As a business woman, I find that compassionate intent is a powerful tool.

The blind broom salesman gave me a gift. He taught me through simple example of his life to be authentic, to trust your Source and to love. I am deeply grateful for his life. When circumstances seem too difficult to bear, or a relationship has left a hole in my heart, I often say to myself, "I choose love". And I am amazed what happens in this release.

***

And so dear reader, what does your heart ache for? Who can you send love to today? What situations are you facing today that could benefit from surrounding it with compassionate intent? How can you create more love in your life, in your family, in your intimate relationships, in your world?

If you follow your bliss, you put yourself on a kind of track, which has been there all the while, waiting for you, and the life that you ought to be living is the one you are living.
-- Joseph Campbell

Post Script:

I never knew his name until recently when I went back to my home town and looked him up 30 years after my first encounter with him. I was amazed to find out he was still alive, in his nineties. I found out his name is Livingston Wills, Yes, I thought it too, a living will. He was born in Tennessee on July 28, 1917. He was the second of eleven children. He began making brooms while in high school at a special factory for the blind. Wanting to attend college, but with no means to do so, he decided to sell brooms to finance his education. Mr. Wills majored in English and History and graduated third in his class of three hundred. He was the only blind man on campus. He wanted to be a teacher, and then he felt this little nudge to become a minister, and although sometimes his congregation in later years amounted to only eight or nine, he would play the piano and deliver a powerful service. For he once said, "wherever two or three are gathered...." It is with deep gratitude

for the life of Livingston Wills that I offer
these principles.

About the Author

Barbara Atkins-Baldwin is a Licensed Practitioner for The United Centers for Spiritual Living. She has her Masters in Jungian Psychology and finds meaning and inspiration in the corporate environment. Her life's purpose is to bridge Spirituality and Business and assist those in finding their true essence and meaning in their work and spiritual life. Her joy comes from being an aunt to her six nieces and nephews. She is a native of Nebraska and now resides in Houston.

Made in the USA
Columbia, SC
08 September 2019